Richard Scarry's
PICTURE
DICTIONARY

Published in Great Britain
with the authorization of Egmont Books
by World International, an imprint of Egmont Publishing Limited,
Egmont House, PO Box 111, Great Ducie Street, Manchester M60 3BL.

Printed in Italy. ISBN 0 7498 1865 4

A catalogue record for this book is
available from the British Library.

note to parents

With the help of Richard Scarry's warm and friendly illustrations, you can help your child learn lots of new words.

In every scene you will find a set of boxes, each with a picture and the name of the object shown below.

You can help your child learn the word, and then find the object in the big picture.

Your child will soon find that it is fun to learn new words! And at the back of the book there is a list of all the objects in alphabetical order.

Richard Scarry's
PICTURE
DICTIONARY

WORLD INTERNATIONAL PUBLISHING LIMITED
MANCHESTER

nightdress

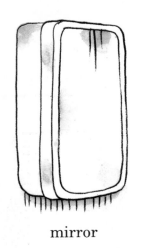

mirror

pyjamas

The bathroom

When Huckle Cat and Sally Cat get up in the morning, they brush their teeth and wash their faces.

All right, Lowly,

how much do you weigh today?

4

comb

hairbrush

soap

shampoo

toothbrush

toothpaste

beaker

towel

talcum powder

bathroom scales

5

underskirt

trousers

handbag

slippers

Sally's room

Sally can't make up her mind what to wear today.
Can you help her?

That's very good, Lowly!
You can tie your shoe!

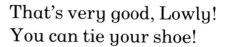

6

jumper

hat

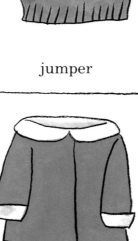

jacket

dress

skirt

shoes

socks

boots

Mother Cat

toy duck

Breakfast time

Huckle, Sally and Lowly have finished eating, but Father Cat is late for breakfast.

window

8

Hurry, Dad, your egg
is getting cold.

9

fork

knife

spoon

napkin

salt and pepper

sugar bowl

milk jug

bacon and eggs

baked beans

cup and saucer

glass of milk

toast

butter

The kitchen

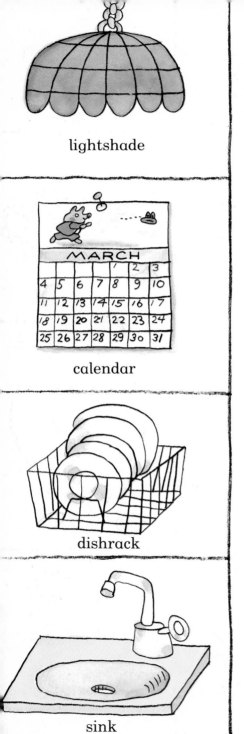

lightshade

calendar

dishrack

sink

You are a good
worker, Lowly.

10

After breakfast, Daddy is doing the dishes.

mug

lemon-squeezer

bowl

teapot

sponge

plate

frying-pan

saucepan

waste-bin

Mother Rabbit
and Baby Rabbit

Goldbug with bulldozer

Postman Pig

SCHOOL BUS

12

The children are on their way to school in Busytown.

Sergeant Murphy helps mother Rabbit to cross the street safely.

13

building brick

motorcycle helmet

whistle

traffic lights

school bus

stop sign

carrot car

Huckle and Lowly on a tricycle

Bananas Gorilla

supermarket with shoppers

Road traffic

Sergeant Murphy is
putting parking tickets
on some cars.

14

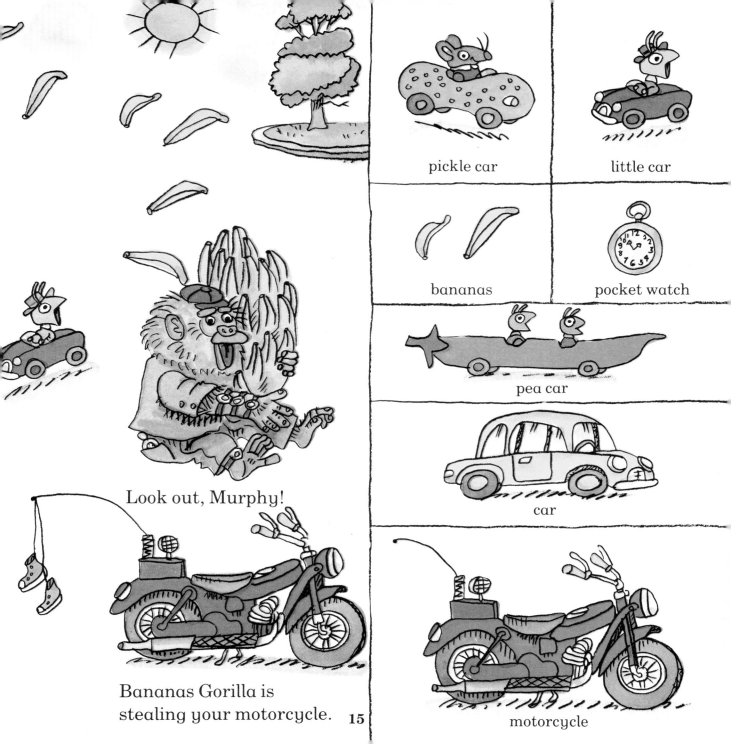

pickle car

little car

bananas

pocket watch

pea car

car

Look out, Murphy!

Bananas Gorilla is
stealing your motorcycle. **15**

motorcycle

picture

Goldbug with paintbrush

Miss Honey the teacher

At school

"Good morning, children," says Miss Honey. "Today is drawing and painting day.

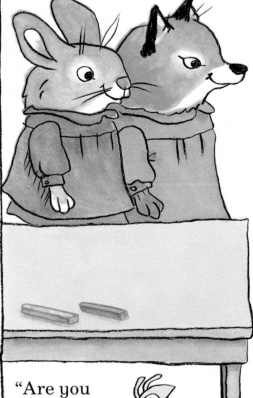

"Are you ready, Goldbug?"

16

" Thank you, Lowly."

17

pencils

eraser

paintbrush

pencil sharpener

paint

crayons

counting rods

paint dish

paper

pen

marker pen

paintbox

spade

bucket

The playground

At break, all the children have a good time playing with their friends.

Goldbug on skates

Sally Cat skipping

18

kite

ball

tricycle

cart

doll

sandpit

19

Delivery Cat

warning sign

hammer   hairbrush

Goldbug with peanut car

Busytown shops

School is over, and the children are helping with the shopping.

SHOEMAK

WET CEMENT

WET CEMENT

Really, Mr Frumble!
Don't you know you must
not walk on the pavement
till the cement is dry?

BARBER

OPEN

scissors

hat

ankle boot

aeroplane

helicopter

eggs

door

Mr Frumble

bicycle

Goldbug with balloon

clock

Mother Mouse
with Baby Mice

Be careful, Mrs Pig.

The supermarket

It is a busy, busy day at the supermarket.

CHOCOLATES

It is such a busy day that nobody has time to wind the clock!

What in the world is Lowly doing in that bag?

23

chocolates

juice

milk

carrot

bread

lettuce

tin

flask

shopping bag

till

trolley

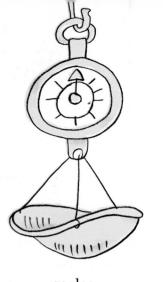

scales

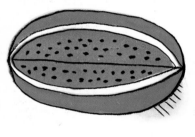

melon

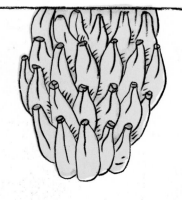

bunch of bananas

The greengrocer

Mother Cat and Sally are buying fruit for dessert tonight.

What is your favourite fruit?

strawberries

apples

oranges

raspberries

pears

grapefruit

bilberries

peaches

lemons

cherries

melons

grapes

basket

carving knife

knife sharpener

mouse with bread

cap

The butcher

What do you think the Cat Family are going to have for dinner tonight?

bacon

sausages

ham

meat cleaver

chop

meat saw

chicken

mincer

garlic sausage

27

window

ladybird

baker's hat

crocodile cake

Baker's shop

Look at all this bread and cake!

Huckle Cat can't
make up his mind.

round loaf

French loaf

tin loaf

cup cakes

pie

iced buns

cherry cakes

chocolate cake

birthday cake

red crayon

orange crayon

yellow crayon

green crayon

blue crayon

purple crayon

What a mess!
Mr Paint Pig has
forgotten to put the
lids on his paint
tins AGAIN.

Please be
more carefu
next time.

Busy Mr Paint Pig

They can see lots of different things on the way home.

Name the colours and find them in the pictures.

red ORANGE yellow

yellow GREEN blue

red PURPLE blue

31

The building site

Jason the mason and Sawdust the carpenter have a lot of help today.

brick wall

barrel of nails

Carpenter Cat

Good work, Goldbug!

hammer

tape measure

nails

set square

bricks

saw

trowel

pipe

ladder

planks

33

tomatoes

cabbages

mouse on bicycle

carrots

On the farm

Farmer Goat is the best farmer ever.

He lives just outside Busytown.

34

cockerel

hen

chick

sack of corn

rake

scythe

tractor

35

At the doctor's

Sally loves to go for
a check-up at Dr Lion's.

She thinks he is the
nicest doctor ever.

Doctor Lion

Nurse Fox

All right, Lowly, how
much do you weigh now?

Get well soon,
Goldbug!

scissors

tweezers

roll of plaster

bandage

tablets

thermometer

sticking plaster

torch

scales

37

The garden

Girl Fly

Boy Fly

hyacinth

daisies

Goldbug with wheelbarrow

hosepipe

Mother Cat likes to work in the garden, and Sally is a very good helper.

Are you?
Greenbug is,
and so is Goldbug.

flower pot

trowel

daffodil

violets

hoe

rake

watering can

39

saw

nails

toy tipper truck

Father Rabbit

In the workshop

Father Rabbit is busy
fixing his son's tricycle.

Thanks for
the help,
Lowly!

40

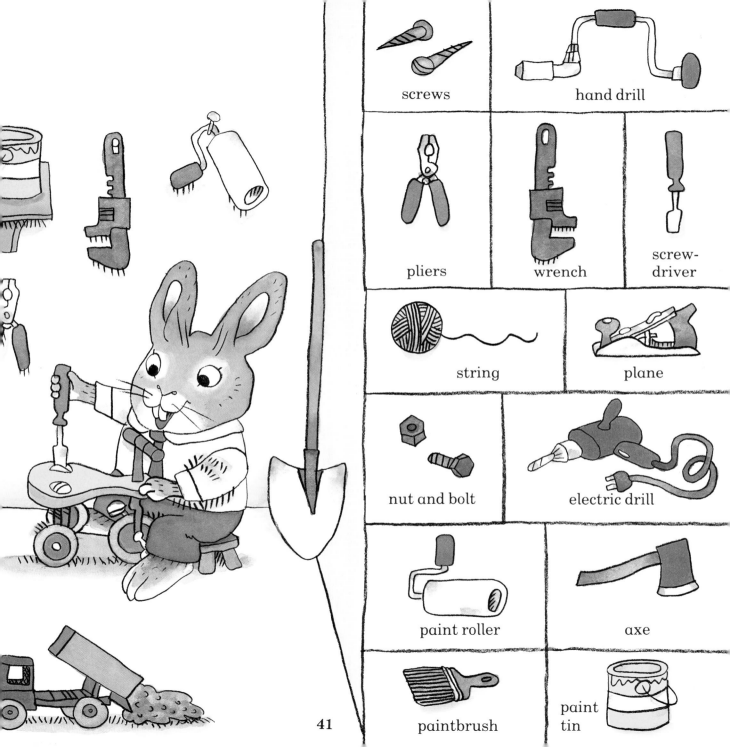

screws

hand drill

pliers

wrench

screw-
driver

string

plane

nut and bolt

electric drill

paint roller

axe

paintbrush

paint
tin

Goldbug with feather duster

helpful Sally Cat

cloud of dust

Cleaning day

Sally and Huckle help
their mother clean the house.

Goldbug wants
to help.

soap

scrubbing brush

broom

cleaning fluid

bucket

vacuum cleaner

43

musical mouse

Goldbug with
ice-cream bulldozer

Huckle Cat with party hat

The birthday party

It is Big Hilda's
birthday today.

All her Busytown friends have come
to wish her Happy Birthday.

streamer

balloons

present

candles

cake

party hats

crackers

45

Word List

Did you name all the things and find them in the pictures?

Here is a list of the objects and the pages you will find them.